PROOF

PROOF

MAGGIE SHAPLEY

RECENT
WORK
PRESS

Proof
Recent Work Press
Canberra, Australia

Copyright © Maggie Shapley 2017

National Library of Australia
Cataloguing-in-Publication entry.
Shapley, Maggie
Proof/ Maggie Shapley

ISBN: 9780995353879 (paperback)

All rights reserved. This book is copyright. Except for private study, research, criticism or reviews as permitted under the Copyright Act, no part of this book may be reproduced, stored in a retrieval system, or transmitted in any form by any means without prior written permission. Enquiries should be addressed to the publisher.

Cover illustration: Image from page 2235 of 'Illinois Agricultural Association record [microform]' (1923)
Cover design: Recent Work Press
Set in Bembo

recentworkpress.com

Contents

Evidence

New Year's Eve	3
Evidence	4
Choice	5
Change	6
Betrayal	7
Googled	8
Blackberry	9
Glebe Point Road	10
Meeting Larkin	11
Alzheimer's	12

Shadow Dance

New Love	15
Morning	16
Weekend in Melbourne	17
Dance	18
Embrace	19
Writing You	20
Reunion	21

Scar Tissue

Scar Tissue	25
Fever	26
Camphor Laurel	27
Riding the Lanes	28
After School	29
Hymns	30
Lake House	31

The Orchardist	32
Auntie Jen	33
Mother in Memory	34
Three Things	35
The Astronomer	36

Time Zones

Flying to Paris	39
Basel	40
Verona	41
Treviso	42
Speaking Italian	43
Border Crossing	44
Venetians	45
Villa d'Este	46
Changdeokgung	47
At Tongdosa	48

Relic

Driving Home	51
Survival Strategy	52
Scattering the Ashes	53
Relic	54
Lunar Eclipse	55
Autumn	56
July	57
The Morning Club	58
At *The White Horse*	59
Death of an Ex	60

Afterword	62

For Sigrid McCausland

We met up on La Rambla and taking the narrow streets faced the surge of an angry demonstration head on. You ducked into a doorway to snap the action and posted it straight to Facebook. Those balmy nights al fresco in ancient courtyards and then the castle, 'the best restaurant in the world' (who knows how they decide that, you say), walking a different way each day on the hunt for quirky museums and modernistas, we chance on locals dancing the sardana—it was a bucket list we didn't know then we were doing.

Evidence

New Year's Eve

Google Earth obscures the numberplate
of my husband's Toyota, perpetually
blocking the driveway of the house we used to share.
I'm standing nearby, impatient arms folded,
waiting, still waiting, for him to drive away.
That New Year's Eve, he insists on a midnight kiss,
like a test of loyalty, a renewal of vows.
Past zero hour I retreat to the garden
listening to the laughter of others,
and witness the well-lit furnished rooms of a life
that isn't mine, like a passenger hovering
above a glittering city in a holding pattern,
waiting for clearance. I walk out on the street
and feel warm rain like permission on my face.

Evidence

The proof is in a single strand of hair:
that is all that's needed to lay the blame,
to name the father, victim or the thief
who tried to leave no fingerprints behind.

The doctor plucked a hair out of my daughter's
unborn head and held it up in tweezers.
'It's a girl' he said, his party-trick, certain
of scientific truth in the midwives' tale.

The white one's my mother's under glass,
the DNA extract shows the fatal gene
for predisposition, grim legacy
for four daughters, and seven more of theirs.

And this hair, blonde from root to tip, lying
on the ensuite floor, not mine or his,
tells another story—
no science to it, just the age-old truth.

Choice

Here, the ocean where all is shift and change,
there, the charted shore, and in between
bright corridor of choice, where questions
niggle at fact, you plant your feet and let
each sucking wave draw you in—what once
so firmly held, sharply-defined, flooded smooth.

That night by water's edge, it wasn't me—
I had swum out beyond the sheltering shore,
knew then what was offered, chose instead
this rough healing, slow drowning, in saltwater.

Change

I mourn for your breadmaking days,
that tense kneading in the dawn light:
slap down on the board,
turn over, and push, push, push,
taste the oven blast,
scorching nostrils and throat.

Today you watch croissants
skate slow around the microwave,
prod them open, and wait
for me to pass the jam.

Betrayal

The sniff of betrayal is all explained away,
now you're the willing accomplice, suggesting a break
and time apart, taking pride in your trusting
flexibility, and he takes up the slack.

Then the irrefutable, the flash,
colour and movement of tawdry circus tricks,
no room for fiction or fast manoeuvring—
you take the full elastic sting, face on.

Googled

I googled my name—the one I was born to
and found my other lives waiting for me:
writing cookbooks with my twin sister,
retired as Town Clerk after 30 years,
another soccer Mom from Virginia,
all plausible alternatives for me.

This seemed a solution to another problem,
and convenient not to change my tattoo,
so I searched for my ex-lover's name
but the Pacific archaeologist,
married, three children in Torrens,
pleaded prior commitment too.

Blackberry

'It's a noxious weed,' her husband had said,
'the currawongs are spreading the fruit to the creek'.
She started early next morning, ambushed it,
secateured the prickly waywardness
into lengths to fit the wheelbarrow,
took the load up the back, as he'd said.
Each cut, she thought of birds returning to feast,
how what you expect doesn't always deliver.
'Consequences, you should think of before
not after,' he'd said, so she thought of him
as she tamed the canes, dug out the roots.
She'd already gathered the fruit and made the jam,
lined up jars on the sink like ammunition,
labelled with the date that would become
the anniversary of leaving him.
It was a blackberry thorn, that festering pain,
sharp in her finger, as she tensed the wheel
and heedless headed out on the highway.

Glebe Point Road

At the local police station
waiting to reclaim a stolen car,
our address shouts across the room
in bolded font on a wanted poster.

Offers a reward for information:
the body of a three-year-old
discarded on a building site
at 268 Glebe Point Road.

It wasn't the same after that,
as if our chosen life was cursed—
knowing the mutilated boy
lay wrapped where we parked the car.

His silent parents—streets from where
we sat sipping G and Ts—
circled by recrimination,
and punishment never matching the crime.

Meeting Larkin

When you arrived for Christmas at the beach,
cantankerous in squinting sun and heat,
I put you aside, and then back-to-work,
everything-in-its-place, you found
your way back home to wait. The weather's turning
cooler, and curious I finger your jacket.
We meet on the page, I read you like a book.

You're the silent observer on a train—
you keep to yourself, not fond of travellers' chat.
You cradle a cryptic crossword as your disguise
while searching the right words, exact and tight,
for who or what flashes blinking past.
Eagle-eyed you watch—seize the prey,
and scribble lines down to play with later.

I would know you better, but you extracted
a promise from your lover to destroy the diaries.
You were silent on the invitations
notated with the date you RSVPed,
filed chronologically in the archives.
Your notebooks, early dated drafts, are there
with their jolting ker-lunk of half-familiar lines.

The poems you didn't send out, detained
like smart-arse adolescents for showing off,
and what you wrote on your rejection slips
incised like beginner's Braille through the page:
'this poem now set for Modern English Verse'.
I'm onto you, inside your glossy cover,
we've met, and you thirty years dead.

Alzheimer's

That summer she insisted on chardonnay
for breakfast—an early sign, or strategy
to blame her confusion on something else?
Strong-willed hard-wired into intransigent,
like a hobby furtively crossing to obsession,
and who-knows-best slipped silently
from parent to child, except neither of us knew,
and the right-thing-to-do eluded us both,
until she punched out her favourite nurse,
the one she said resembled her daughter.

Today I'm her sister lost at sea
in the war, before I was born.
It's taken me this long to swim to Java,
recover from amnesia, and trade my body
for passage on the steamer—she's thought this through
the rough justice of her brain. I don't let on,
try to recall the childhood stories she told me
to reminisce about our days at school.
She wanders off, switches on the television—
sometimes she sees her daughter on the news.

Shadow Dance

New Love

On nights like tonight I float on my back in the sea,
lapping up the rock of the waves, the pinch
of saltwater drying on my skin,
the flutter of hands keeping me afloat.

Is this how it would be or is this just for now?
Would each day start here on the beach, and end
with sea breeze caressing though my hair?
Or would I grow complacent—the occasional stroll
on the sand after work, forgetting the tides?

A wave distracts and I am upright again:
open my eyes, plant my feet on the sand,
and will my thighs to wade back to shore.

Morning

Every other time there's been a deadline.
'I really must be getting back', you've said
and left around an hour after that.
But now it's morning and not a word.
We're lying in bed, the curtains pushed wide,
watching the rose bushes twitch in the rain,
aware of all outside our usual selves.
'It's like this every morning', I say.
I mean either this or the sun lights up
the cobwebs bright with dew, or the sky
blushes through the drab of the gum tree,
or after the magpies' choir the currawongs
chase away the wattle birds. I mean
the only thing that's different is you've stayed.

Weekend in Melbourne

The smell cities have after rain
sweeter than compost, oil-streaked,
heady as jasmine, seduces us
to march in step on black wet streets

in search of food. Outstepping spruikers
on Lygon Street we're free to choose
Nepalese washed down
with boutique red. Head to head

at the bookshop still hungry for words
you feed me in low whispers—
knowing loss, I hoard these crusts
and buy ten books for later.

Espressos thick with sugar sticks,
we sip, sip, sip like bees and sleep
content, windows open, in tune
with the traffic's splash and hum.

Dance

The way he gets into a car,
unfolds, holding his jacket flat
at the front, a player protecting
vulnerable parts from penalty kick,
like the slow shadow dance we do,
the formal bow and step, holding
in check the fond and forbidden words
until minuet turns flamenco
with only glance and tilt of head
predicting the stamp of feet, thrust
and knock of bones, the naked shout,
then the true words barely spoken
brush from lips, dance along fingers,
settle on skin and catch in our hair.

Embrace

My head still full of salty seaweed,
this sudden embrace surprises, the constant
shush of the ocean demands my silence.
Later, alone, breathing in
the stalky-dry wheat-chaff air,
I see the intention, and careful with words,
frame a spontaneous reply
that speaks of situation more than love.

Writing You

Writing you into this place
requires a heavenly transposition:
the sun to set below the ocean
and rise behind the scrubby dunes—
import the whitest sand,
wheel in screeching gulls
to recreate your memory of a beach.

Or you're hiding here in metaphor—
the urgent persistence of ocean,
an undercurrent, or a wave
that staggers up the beach saying
'don't expect too much of me'.
To write you here, in your absence,
is to imagine anything is possible.

Reunion

Rehearse an anxious scan of waiting faces
before recognition throws its shaft
of light eye-to-eye in electric focus,
laughing, you turn your head as I feign surprise.
Will this future in its variations
unravel, undone by being brought to mind?

Instead, picture you awkward and tongue-tied,
nervous, bringing gaudy, gushing flowers—
or strolling in late, you introduce your wife:
I forget your name and absently inspect
my glossy nails as if for inspiration.
How could the truth be stranger than this?

Scar Tissue

Scar Tissue

A crucifix is centred on my forehead
like a blessing from a priestly thumb,
sign of the cross concealed within the furrow,
milky intersection of stitch and incision.

Forbidden short-cut through the building site,
new brickwork's biting roughness grazed my cheek,
a fresh-laid corner caught me between the eyes.
My sister, seven, knew the score, instructed
'it was the fence, you climbed through it: say it!'
Reluctant to say that wood could wound like this,
blurt out the blood that dripped across my sleeve,
'OK, the fence—the sharp edge of the post'.

A lesson learnt: when you lie, you spin
your own web—you need to keep repeating,
more foolish every time. 'It seems unlikely',
the doctor said, looping his waxed black thread.
Three stitches, and made to walk the long way round.

Each morning the mirror recalls the lie my mother
died believing. A week before, she touched my face,
'remember, you cut your forehead on the fence?'
Reluctant to trespass on the lucid thought,
'yes, the fence, walking home from school'.

Fever

Nine years old, struck with scarlet fever,
I clutched the cool chrome of the bedhead
to counteract my body's excess heat,
repositioning hands as metal warmed.
Diagnosed with brain-addling delirium
or perhaps a crucifixion complex,
I kept faith in my own logic,
stubbornly clung to my resolve.
Now in the fevered grip of hot flush,
mobile phone pressed against my cheek,
I remember every pore alert
to the slightest motion of clammy air,
the stream of sweat as the fever broke
and the exquisite shiver as it left.

Camphor Laurel

This house now seems impossibly small
for seven of us, 'almost a cricket team',
even with two extensions squaring off
the cricket pitch where Mum planted the spindly
camphor laurel against the westerly sun.

It did for cricket stumps except she'd water
and muddy the crease, where we'd mark out our line
like Chappell did on TV. When Jim was clean-bowled,
just the once, branches and curses flew:
she declared the game over, the pitch out-of-bounds.

Thirty years later, the wicket blossoms
in extravagant clusters over the tiles,
shading the room where all of us slept in bunks,
outside, a battered abandoned bat leans
against the regulation-width trunk.

Riding the Lanes

Riding our bikes after school was a way to escape piano practice and the roster of chores. We'd call out 'we're just going around the block' then head for the old part of town where pot-holed lanes split the long blocks of houses and shops—back gates opened to private spaces, colourful washing on the line, empty bottles in wooden crates, and dishevelled women who looked up quickly to see who it was, as if they expected someone else, but we were just kids on our bikes, so they took another drag on their cigarette and looked the other way, as we swerved around the overflowing garbage cans and splashed through the muddy-water puddles, our thonged feet high as the handle-bars.

After School

My job to chop the wood
and stoke the evening fire,
my sister's to shovel the coke
for the breakfast stove.
Hers didn't take as long,
but when we swapped the once,
black grit gripped my throat.

I preferred the hour outside,
trusted to swing the axe:
the dead thunk that echoed
off the rusty shed,
the warm ooze of resin,
the splintery brickwork stack
slowly filling the barrow.

One day I found a rabbit,
quivering fur wedged
in a dead-end hollow:
inched the blade to split
the log apart—it lay
dead still, stiff-eared,
panting, before it bolted.

At dinner, it sounded like
too much imagination—
'stowaway rabbits?
what's next?'—months later
my sister unshovelled a body,
the escapee imprisoned,
tunnelled into black dust.

Hymns

On Saturday nights my father chose the hymns.
All afternoon he'd labour over the sermon,
tackling the Bible text and teasing out
what it meant for his country congregation,
while other people's fathers watched the football.
He'd say 'the message is all about redemption,
we need some hymns that run along those lines'.
Mum would offer suggestions: 'How great Thou art'
or 'number 92 that has that verse
about the cleansing of the sinners' souls?'
She'd sing the first few lines while washing up—
her contralto clear above my father's baritone
reverberating through the warmth of the kitchen.
Then one of us would run the list of numbers
up the road—the spinster who played the organ
would quickly check for unfamiliar tunes.
Next morning my mother's songs were taken up
and delivered in full accompanied chorus.

Lake House

There's no nostalgia here, no hint of it,
except the message whispered by the wind
through the shredded bark of the single gum,
towering over the terrace, shedding leaves
into the pool all year long.

Near the new jacuzzi, by new palms
transplanted from the north, a girl once sat,
knees bent to fit the window seat, reading
of other worlds, far from the Lake house,
waiting for the southerly.

Behind the newly laid brick, the swaying
house of memory remains, its deceptive planks
and warped weatherboard reminding you
that nothing keeps—life's uncertain journey:
racing canoes ahead of the storm.

The Orchardist

'Like this', he said, turning the orange into the blade,
the snakeskin falling to the ground,
a saucer of rind to catch the juice
cupped in his calloused hand.
'Here, take my spare—don't tell your Mum—
you never know when you'll need it,
until you leave your knife at home.'
We only saw him once a year—
there was something the adults never said
that fuelled the mystery about him:
he had that country way of standing,
reading the weather in the clouds and hills.
He drove the ute into the bush one time
and took a rifle 'in case there's a fox'
to show off his treasure, a waratah in flower.
Later at uni, when offered whisky,
I smelt his throaty chuckle and remembered
the nicotine stains on his fingers,
as he twirled the magic orange in his hand.

Auntie Jen

'We can't always have what we want,'
she said, stretching out her shrivelled arm
to clasp my shoulder's smooth tan,
'sometimes we have to do their bidding'.
This, after my father, her nephew,
vetoed my plans—it was clear who *they* were.
Her good hand strong in consolation,
I took comfort it wouldn't be this way again

My great-aunt Jen lived in the house
she was born in, with her bed-ridden sisters,
still mourning their brother and her lover
who hadn't returned from the Somme,
strong from lifting bodies from bed to chair
and a lifetime of sewing men's suits by hand.

Mother in Memory

You won't be caught with idle hands,
you're podding the peas or stringing the beans
or tying your apron behind your back.
I try to recall you reading a book
but you won't be captured this way.
Country-born, making-do,
giving hospitality
before it was an industry,
you were flummoxed by city ways.
'Let them get on with it,' you'd say.
You met two childhood ambitions:
to marry and wear your hair in a bun.
Our conversation often faltered,
skirting what to you was right and true
to find the safe common ground:
the constant, restless doing and making,
inherited like a mutant gene.

Three Things

'The fridge, the plumber and the kangaroo,
that's three things, you're safe', my daughter said,
'bad things always come in threes'.

It's true—the fridge expired and blew the fuse,
the plumber left a cataclysmic bill,
and today the kangaroo's body blow,
five hundred dollars of excess to pay.

'But when do you start the count?' I said, 'what if
the plumber was number three, because the fridge
was number two and something else came first?
What if there's two more kangaroos?'

'But then it wouldn't work', she said, her eyebrows
arched in disbelief, 'you wouldn't be safe—
the last bad thing is always number three'.

The Astronomer

The nurse whose job it was to tie the ends
returned his wallet to his waiting child:
the worn-out leather recalled the childhood smell
of books deliberately out of reach
containing things she wouldn't understand.
Inside, a familiar hand on feint-lined paper:
his name, street, town and state, 'Australia,
The Earth, The Solar System, The Universe'.
A summary stark with possibility,
begging addition of what remained unknown.
The daughter remembered his quizzing interrogation
about the smallest truth, as if the answer
always lay in magnifying detail,
expanding concentrated pricks of light,
and the gaze that veered ever upwards
beyond the provenance of earthly things.

Time Zones

Flying to Paris

Don't fly business class unless someone else pays:
spend the difference at Galeries Lafayette.
Book a seat at the rear of the plane—it's safer
'in the unlikely event of a catastrophe'
and your best chance for a nearby empty seat.
Order vegetarian to get served first.
Congratulate yourself for being short,
all that extra legroom free of charge.

Use the hours ahead productively:
contemplate your life, see how paltry
your problems are, already time zones away.
Watch a movie—expect no adult themes—
all rated G for Guaranteed to please.
Play nineteen games of spider solitaire.
Read four pages of a fat paperback,
before you fall into a drunken doze.

Wake to a baby's cries. Glare at the mother:
make sure she knows how inconvenienced you are.
Breakfast at 4 pm Eastern Standard Time.
On arrival, chat to your neighbours—
now's a good time to get to know them.
Race your companions to the passport queue,
update your Facebook status to say 'In Paris',
then wait for your luggage for an hour or two.

Basel

It's unseasonably warm in Basel
and forty years since we were lovers—your voice
is just the same, your words familiar,
then in staccato German you order the coffee.
I'm only here for a day with my daughter
who might have been yours—you think so too,
scanning the curve of her back, the turn of her head.
Your kids are much younger, and your wife,
'Achtung!' she says and we all pull up short:
it's for the boy—a tram's crossing the platz.
We barter brief words about our common past,
I've misremembered our anniversary
but you know the date. It was a bet between us
back then—who would forget the other one first.

Verona

The world stands still in Basilica di San Zeno:
the crypt is a forest of Romanesque columns
where monstrous creatures entwine the capitals
and frescoes reach out their hands in ancient blessing.
The faintest touch on my shoulder slides
tantalisingly across my back,
strokes my arm, until he sees my face.
I am not his wife. Profuse apologies,
my own assurances that this was nothing more
than the body press of a peak-hour bus—
I raise a single finger to my lips
to say conspiratorially 'it's our secret'
but he won't be drawn in, steps away
and retreats into his own embarrassment.

Treviso

Treviso brings to mind your life at home—
not the arches enclosing marble footpaths
trodden smooth by centuries of strolling feet,
not the well-dressed women cycling slow
along crooked streets with lofted umbrellas,
not the Roman mosaic under the piazza
where smiling guides point out to English tourists
the jagged line marking Allied bombing
below the reconstructed Venetian windows,
not the bronzes dug out of ancient mud
glowing in spotlights at the civic museum
where one century's frescoes obscure another's:
the virgin overlooks the shoulder of Christ
and Saint Ursula shakes the hand of the pope,
not the city walls where dogwalkers strut
past entangled lovers monopolising benches,
not the rough-hewn beam you sleep beneath,
branches slashed as if yesterday
the trunk was plucked upright from primal forest,
no—it's the familiar whine of mosquitoes
rising from the canal that takes you back—
they lurk in curtains, anchored down by blood,
despatched with a clap, a splash of red on your palm.

Speaking Italian

Thrown back to childhood, my first telephone call,
hanging up the heavy black handpiece
to stop the impenetrable flow of chatter.
Instead, 'scusi, non parlo italiano'
to parry the words that collide and come too fast,
and refuse to resemble what I expected in reply.
Maria interprets, 'she thinks she speaks Italian
but it's dialect—she says it's best
to see Venice at night' and rolls her eyes.
Her mother-in-law has come for Sunday lunch,
holds up toys for grandchildren one-by-one:
'telefono, il treno, l'autobus'—
at last, these are words I understand.

Border Crossing

Line markings switch from white to luminous yellow, tall trees fall away to tussocky grass, high beam scans for wild horses crossing, hydroelectric powerlines diverge across the highway and disappear into night, our mobile phones are silenced. We turn off and snake along the dirt track as far as it goes. Our conversation clangs against the walls until the stove is lit. Outside, the moon almost full, the night air the promise of tomorrow's snow.

Venetians

In Nafplio your style is on show,
each house, the wrought-iron balcony,
the portico arching afternoon shade,
the winged lion ruling iron-strapped doors.

Beneath the fortress you built above the town
you swam with local olive-skinned girls,
followed their swaying skirts past the church,
and caught up to them in shaded groves.

You left your lion-stamp there as well.
Even now above the playground chant
conquisto—the Venetian cry—rings out.
A red-headed boy loiters in the square,
drums his football against the stuccoed wall
until each foreign brick is conquered again.

Villa d'Este

In the room with mirrored walls, we danced with words, catching sunlit glimpses of ourselves as we sashayed and side-stepped and spun. Exuberance spent, we stepped out on the terrace to test our phrasing, the humid air held us close till words found their right places, and the sky widened with the possibility of other rooms, the perennial thought of abundant gardens to explore on other days. Out of the silence, the bright murmur of your voice, 'I am here, I am here, I am here', a string of amber beads around my neck.

Changdeokgung

In the secret garden the king provided
pavilions for poets, straddling land and lake,
to contemplate the maples' changing light,
the shape of water-lilies and mountain rock,
the juniper's thousand years of branching out.

The palace guide explains the harmony
propitious for the dual art: the composing
and the calligraphy—how thought will sketch
about the page and meaning gather its strands
within each inky stroke of tapered brush.

'The bright square of pond is man's invention,
inside, Nature's island of weeping trees,
that's the yin and yang', she says, 'this garden,
where our exertions meet the gravelled earth,
exhibits the essence of Korean philosophy'.

The same, if you scaled the palace wall
guarding this kept remnant of fissured trees,
you'd see the neon advertisements written
on apartment blocks as grand as palaces,
the shadowed bright and dark in harmony.

At Tongdosa

She grabs my hand and drags me through the gate,
the flow of foreign words only later
understood: 'This way, the food is free
for Buddha's birthday—pay-back time for monks'.

We eat another lunch to satisfy
her generosity—no place for leftovers,
we finish our soup and wash and stack our bowls.
Spongy green bread is pressed in our hands.

My great-grandfather swam in the river
after a sleepless night in an airless room—
the hospitality repaid with cake,
the monks assured no butter would pass their lips.

The river's clear to the rounded rocks beneath,
in remembrance I pick up a greenish stone,
and realise later my memento's not jade,
but whitest marble covered in ancient moss.

Relic

Driving Home

Driving home from my mother's funeral
I get another speeding ticket. 'My daughters—
I must get back—there's so little time',
but the policeman's much too young
to register mortality. 'My husband,'
I should have said, 'tore his hamstring at football'.
Better to lie, than implicating her
in a conversation she never would have had.

Today we emptied all your dresser drawers
and I reclaimed the scarves you kept for good
and the small flat tin of poems you'd cut
from newspapers—I can't ask you now
what you saved them for: can't ring and tell you
what happened today, driving home.

Survival Strategy

Death has stolen my address book,
scores through names, uncouples,
tears out the pages where
gilt edges spread open
and I rang to say he'd gone.

Now I reconstruct:
hide my precious ones
in crisp pages crammed
with every brief acquaintance,
each one living dangerously.

Scattering the Ashes

'There must be a poem in this', she said.
'Last month, she was implacable, petulant:
today, released into pure still light.'
We followed her instructions—half on the beach,
half near the spreading tree on the back nine—
divided up beforehand to get it right,
anticipating the greedy gust of wind
eager to claim more than its share.
This morning's fiery sunrise—it's her you know—
not a heavenly star, benignly guiding
future lives (an unlikely transformation),
but in each day's dawning over the sea
in this rosy cloud of dust caught
between the sun and earthly eyes, she glows.

Relic

Wet strands of hair on folded arms
in classic Dupain sunbaker pose,
I lick the saltwater from my wrist
and taste fifty hot summers past.

We came here first as lovers, oblivious
to witnesses to our water games,
then as parents staking out our patch
with cupped warning shouts and cricket stumps.

By myself, I'm becoming invisible,
haunting this silent towel's-width space,
disowning the wizened skin on my hands
and withered thighs: a relic of another time.

As I leave, the beddable young man
offers instead to carry my beach umbrella,
I blame my tears on the sun's glare
and memories of you swimming naked in the sea.

Lunar Eclipse

It's only vaguely orange, not the blood
the ancients saw, the wrath of Saxon gods,
or is it my perception that has paled,
eroded by spectacle and neon light?

Still an irresistible power tugs,
the thin silver slice of moon succumbs,
dims to the rusty light, and then despite
everything I know and commonsense,

I raise my chardonnay and make a wish
to the round orange moon-god, disregard
the neighbours' nosy curtains, and moon-struck,
dance a tarantella, traitor to my age.

Autumn

The Chinese pistachio tree taunts
with its flickering flame-red leaves
and the pin-oaks lie in wait
on the turn from summer green.
The usual remedies seem to fail—
pressing spidery roots in soil,
pruning dead wood from the rose,
raspberries eaten straight from cane—
then a seed of consolation
inserts itself between eye and brain:
ten thousand red flags celebrate
the change of season, trumpet the arrival
of daffodil shoots pushing through,
and the sky a blaze of bluest blue.

July

Frost sharpens every blade of grass
so there's no mistaking the truth of things.
Each serrated edge and feathered vein
reveals what is mapped in the master plan.
Further off, the early promise of wattle
hovers in eucalyptus blue haze,
but now a dead rosella, crimson still green,
foretells the death of love before it blooms.

The Morning Club

'Morning', we say, even though we're strangers—
our one thing in common: we got up early,
ahead of household and kids and escaped for a walk
with the dog on leash, if we've got one.

There's the guy with headphones and heelers attached,
the fitness freak strident in fluoro stripes
who's focused on destination, the woman my age,
twice my size, disguised in purple caftan.

A familiar face without a dog—'Morning,
where's Rolf?', I say, before I meet her eyes.
She's had him put down—I'm not the first to ask
and console, but still don't know her name.

'Best time of the day', he always says as we pass.
I imagine us as lovers—how we'd conspire
a complete unnoticed hour of intimacy
on the pretext of the benefits of exercise.

Later at the shops we're embarrassed by recognition—
our knowledge of faces, of tears too early in the day,
the compulsion we share to walk alone at dawn,
what poems and schemes we churn in our heads.

At *The White Horse*

Before she got to us, her tight grey perm,
she must have tottered through the public bar,
her crimplene dress, her orthopaedic shoes,
negotiated the row of vinyl stools,
the rusty sandtrays spiked with orange butts,
the lino laid in the late sixties' boom,
across the foyer, its cigarette machine
crowded round by furtive uniforms,
schoolkids dodging the barmaid's line of sight,
into the ladies' lounge, where we'd brought
our drinks for privacy, her hurried steps
heading for the ladies' loo, she stopped
mid-stride, alert, defeated. The hot stream
hissed into the red and purple carpet—
we turned our heads askance, the sharp smell,
a full minute, until unsteady footsteps,
shuffling, less urgent, resumed their destination,
her swaying body awkward in retreat,
and my companion, bursting, laughed out loud.

No need to fear the final nodding off,
the silent cluster of familial concern,
but beware the sniggering clutch of bystanders,
the torture rack of slow unravelling—
scant testimony of wide-eyed lovers
and teenagers buying their first pack of fags.

Death of an Ex

My place is in the second tier of grief,
the former wife of a newly-married man,
outside the inner circle that lingers for closure,
while willing it not to happen just yet.

Hearing his diagnosis, I stammer out
an apology, but there's no need he says,
'otherwise I wouldn't have met my soulmate.
No offence, but now I'm happy at last'.

I stalk his illness on Facebook, discover
he's joined 'Your Not My Ex, Your My Mistake'.
I'm more affronted by how it's spelt, retreat
from his request to become a friend.

Days later, I sit at the front
between our daughters. A celebrant recasts
his life, edits out our twenty years,
as photographs I took flash on screen.

The coffin chugs from the chapel accompanied
by Queen, 'Another one bites the dust'.
I'm a stranger at the wrong funeral
who no-one knows, but no-one asks to leave.

Afterword

I've always lived with strings of words—words I've read or conversations, real or imaginary—running through my head. At university I discovered Chaucer, and Anglo-Saxon poetry with its two-beat half-lines linked by alliteration rather than rhyme. I spent months translating *Beowulf* and then a 15th-century chronicle, working from the original manuscript. The archaic rhythms of those words and the power of direct speech wormed themselves into my brain.

As an archivist I have a professional obsession with evidence and a forensic attention to detail, particularly to the meaning and placement of words. It was only in my forties that I started to tame and reconstruct my words into poetry. My poems may sometimes read as autobiography, but for me, poetry is fiction, although there is always a germ of truth—a starting point in my life from which the words begin their journey.

Acknowledgements

'Evidence' was published in *Westerly* and *The Best Australian Poetry 2004* (University of Queensland Press), 'Change' in *Poetrix*, 'Choice', 'Survival Strategy' and 'Lake House' in *Kalimat*, 'Googled' in the *Canberra Times*, 'Driving Home' in *ACTWrite* and *Winners* (Ginninderra Press), 'The Morning Club' in *Blast*, 'Lunar Eclipse' and 'July' in *Muse*, 'After School' in *Block*, and 'At Tongdosa' in *Cordite*. 'Driving Home' won the 2003 ACT Writers Centre Poetry Award, 'Changdeokgung' was shortlisted in the 2008 ArtsACT David Campbell Award and 'Camphor Laurel' for the 2009 Cricket Poetry Prize. 'New Year's Eve' and 'Scar Tissue' were short-listed in the 2013 Jean Cecily Drake-Brockman Poetry Prize and together with 'Blackberry' and 'The Orchardist' were published in *Long Glances: A snapshot of new Australian poetry* (Manning Clark House). 'Villa d'Este' was published in *Pulse: Prose Poems,* Recent Work Press, Canberra, 2016. In 2007 I received an ArtsACT grant which enabled me to travel to Korea and write a number of poems.

I am grateful to the editors of these journals and collections, and to Shane Strange of Recent Work Press, for publishing my poems, and thank my friends and family for their encouragement, in particular my daughters Kate and Alex Shapley, Margaret Innes, Stephanie Haygarth, and Paul Hetherington.

Maggie Shapley is a Canberra poet and University Archivist at the Australian National University. She won the 2003 ACT Writers Centre Poetry Award and her poems have been published in literary journals, anthologies and on Canberra buses in the Poetry in Action series from 2007 to 2009. Most recently she's writing prose poems on her phone as part of the Prose Poetry Project at the University of Canberra.

2016 Editions

Pulse **Prose Poetry Project**
Incantations **Subhash Jaireth**
Transit **Niloofar Fanaiyan**
Gallery of Antique Art **Paul Hetherington**
Sentences from the Archive **Jen Webb**
River's Edge **Owen Bullock**

2017 Editions

A Song, the World to Come **Miranda Lello**
Cities: Ten Poets, Ten Cities **Various**
The Bulmer Murder **Paul Munden**
Dew and Broken Glass **Penny Drysdale**
Members Only **Melinda Smith and Caren Florance**
the future, un-imagine **Angela Gardner and Caren Florance**
Proof **Maggie Shapley**
Black Tulips **Moya Pacey**
Soap **Charlotte Guest**
Isolator **Monica Carroll**
Ikaros **Paul Hetherington**
Work & Play **Owen Bullock**

all titles available from
www.recentworkpress.com

www.ingramcontent.com/pod-product-compliance
Lightning Source LLC
Chambersburg PA
CBHW020624300426
44113CB00007B/774